Baruntse

Above 7000 metres in the Himalayas

Bo Belvedere Christensen climbing in the Eastern part of Nepal
Photo by Jan Mathorne

Baruntse

Above 7000 metres in the Himalayas

By

Bo Belvedere Christensen

Also by the author (all titles in danish):

Ama Dablam - en bestigning af verdens smukkeste bjerg, medforfatter, Gyldendal 1989.

Everest - drømmen og sejren, redaktør og medforfatter, Jyllandsposten forlag 2000.

Baruntse - over 7000 meter i Himalaya, BoD 2008.

Big E - fortællingen om Big E Thrane & Thrane Danish Everest Expedition 2000, 132 pages, BoD 2008.

Ubetrådte tinder - gennem hvide pletter på landkortet til toppen af jomfruelige toppe i Himalaya, 120 pages, BoD 2008.

Kilimanjaro - Guide til natur og bestigning, BoD 2009.

Vertikalt - noveller om klatring og bjergbestigning, BoD 2009.

De smukke bjerge - Gasherbrum gruppen i Pakistan, BoD 2010.

Klatring i Peru - på udfordrende tinder i Andesbjergene, BoD 2011

© 2011 Bo Belvedere Christensen

Publisher: Books on Demand GmbH, Copenhagen, Denmark

Print: Books on Demand GmbH, Norderstedt, Germany

Cover: Bo Belvedere Christensen

Photos: Bo Belvedere Christensen

ISBN: 978-87-7114-250-1

Contents

PREFACE — 8

A CHAOTIC BEGINNING — 9

ACCLIMATISATION — 11

BARUNTSE — 22

GOING HOME OR? — 34

CLOSING THE RING — 43

EXPEDITION SUMMARY — 48

FACTS ON THE AUTHOR — 51

List of illustrations

Figure 1: Overview of Mera Peak *10*

Figure 2: Overview of Nepal with the expediton area marked *10*

Figure 3: The view up through the Khumbu valley from near to Pangkongma *11*

Figure 4: Camp in Pangkongma *11*

Figure 5: The group in front of Mera Peak at the bottom of the valley *12*

Figure 6: Camp in Nashing Dingma *12*

Figure 7: Jesper on one of our acclimatisation climbs *13*

Figure 8: Head shaped rock pillar near Chalem Kharka *13*

Figure 9: The beautiful and difficult mountain TangTse *13*

Figure 10: Camp in Khare, the socalled basecamp *14*

Figure 11: Hanging glacier on TangTse *14*

Figure 12: The two highest Mera summits, the central summit in the middle, North to the right *15*

Figure 13: On route up the last part of the Mera glacier *15*

Figure 14: Many glacier have a steep edge. The Mera glacier is no exception *16*

Figure 15: A few hours after the start from Mera High Camp *16*

Figure 16: Martin, Jens, and Jesper on Mera with Everest behind and Baruntse to the right .. *17*

Figure 17: Jesper at the crevasse below the summit wall on Mera Central *17*

Figure 18: Lhakpa dancing for victory on Mera Central *18*

Figure 19: Martin, Bo, Jesper and Jens on Mera North. Baruntse behind us to the right *18*

Figure 20: Anny and Dachhamba on the last part against the summit *19*

Figure 21: Bo and Anny on the summit of Mera North *19*

Figure 22: Martin and Jens on the way to West Col during a snow shover *20*

Figure 23: Martin on the snow covered moraine with Baruntse and Baruntse II in the background ... *20*

Figure 24: Baruntse basecamp. West Col, Baruntse and Baruntse II behind. *21*

Figure 25: West Col, where the route crossed just to the right of the leftmost rocks. *22*

Figure 26: The view towards Makalu from camp 1 .... *22*

Figure 27: Jens and Martin by camp 1 in the West Col *23*

Figure 28: Jens and Martin on the way towards camp 2 .... *23*

Figure 29: Climbers from our group on their way at dawn *24*

Figure 30: The summit attempt takes place in sunny weather with only a few clouds *24*

Figure 31: Starting from the col betwen Baruntse and Baruntse II *25*

Figure 32: Jens on fixed ropes at around 6600 metres. Baruntse II just behind him to the left *25*

Figure 33: Anny and Dachhamba on fixed ropes *26*

Figure 34: The scary soft ridge where we turned around in 6900 metres *26*

Figure 35: The group in Baruntse Basecamp before the summit attempt *27*

Figure 36: Baruntse II gennem teleobjektivet fra Basecamp *27*

Figure 37: Jens and Martin in the small icefall between camp 1 and 2 .... *28*

Figure 38: On the way up the Southeast ridge of Baruntse on beautiful morning *28*

Figure 39: Jens on the way to Baruntse *29*

Figure 40: Martin takes a deserved brake beneath a serac wall on the way to Baruntse *29*

Figure 41: Anny and Dachhamba on their way with Makalu in the background *30*

Figure 42: The big drop to the valley where Basecamp is located *30*

Figure 43: Going up the thin edge of the ridge on Baruntse at 6800 metres *31*

Figure 44: Martin on his way up the ridge of Baruntse II *31*

Figure 45: Martin and Jens near the summit of Baruntse II. "Big" Baruntse behind *32*

Figure 46: The author, Bo Belvedere Christensen, on the summit of Baruntse II 32

Figure 47: The big unstable ice cake that made us abandon the summit on Baruntse 33

Figure 48: Afternoon clouds are covering the valley but not the lakes to the left of which Basecamp is located. 33

Figure 49: Climbers as small dots on their way up the summit ridge of Baruntse 35

Figure 50: A beautiful evening in Basecamp and a new chance to get to the summit 35

Figure 51: Lhakpa carrying his backpack with straps and band across his forehead 36

Figure 52: A lightly clouded morning we start our second summit attempt on Baruntse 36

Figure 53: Lhakpa and Pemba, two faithful helpers 37

Figure 54: The ridge shortly before our previous high point 37

Figure 55: Just passed the gap in the snowridge marked by a traversion crevasse 39

Figure 56: Martin on the short vertical section of the ridge 39

Figure 57: We believe to be looking at the summit at the right, but nothing is certain 40

Figure 58: Martin on the last part of the snow ridge 40

Figure 59: The broad final ridge, now we know we will make it 41

Figure 60: Bo, Martin and Jens on the summit of Baruntse 41

Figure 61: Jens on the summit of Baruntse 42

Figure 62: Martin on the summit of Baruntse 42

Figure 63: Bo on the summit of Baruntse, in the background the Everest group looms 43

Figure 64: Three happy sherpas on the summit of Baruntse: Lhakpa, Pemba and Balbadur 43

Figure 65: Some of the climbers from the english team on the last steep part of the climb to Baruntse 45

Figure 66: Baruntse BC by night 46

Figure 67: Dachhamba on his way to Amphu Laptsa with the terraced glacier behind 46

Figure 68: A view from Amphu Laptsa 47

Figure 69: The view towards where we are descending from the Amphu Laptsa pass 47

Figure 70: At Dingboche we are passing below the extremely beautiful mountain Ama Dablam ,, ... 48

Figure 71: Sometimes you get so tired ... Anny at the end of the expedition 48

Figure 72: Route diagram 50

Figure 73: Altitude curve with day and night altitudes 50

Figure 74: Bo Belvedere Christensen in the hot southern France 52

Preface

The spring 2008 was rather chaotic for travellers to Tibet due to the prelude to the Olympic Games in Beijing. It created demonstrations and unrest far into the mountain areas. In the area where we, from Kipling Travel, had planned an expedition, Tibet became prohibited land. Nevertheless we ended up having a wonderful expedition, where many goals were achieved, many limits were explored although the goals ended up being something quite from what we originally imagined.

The mountain areas of Nepal, Tibet, Pakistan and many other Himalayan places has long since attracted me strongly. Most of the times I've been there has been on climbing expeditions but I've also bagged a couple of nice trekking trips. I've always entered with a feeling of coming home and left the area for me real home in Denmark with a feeling of loss. Every time I'm going for another expedition I'm looking much forward to experiencing the beautiful nature and the friendly local people.

I've travelled in the Himalayas with a lot of different companions but in the later years I've primarily worked as expedition leader for Kipling Travel. This has not in any way diminished my joy. The experience has been different but in many aspects even more intense. When I'm travelling as leader of a group, the requirement is that I'm on top of the task at all times. It cannot stretch me to my own limit. Naturally, the higher and more challenging the mountains become the less the surplus of mental and physical resources will be. It is partially for this reason that Kipling cooperates with a local agent in Nepal. They ensure we have skilled local guides that contribute to the security and the chance of success. The company, Explore Himalaya, have a lot of guides associated - guides that travel in the mountains every year and every season. They have a thorough local knowledge of the areas we want to visit. Should it happen that Explore Himalaya doesn't have a guide with enough knowledge of the zone we want to visit, they are willing to hire one from another company in Kathmandu..

This way we are always certain before leaving for the Himalayas that we have a team that will assure the best experience. Furthermore, that we get exactly the challenge we seek and meet it prepared in the best way. The local guides guarantees the highest possible chance of succes and safety. I have only positive praise for the strong team that assisted us on the experience described in this book. They gave us all possible support and did everything within their powers to make us feel comfortable and ready to meet the challenges.

In this short book I've gathered the experience from the trip, collected facts of the expedition and documented some of it with my own photographs. I hope that this book will function as an appetizer for others who might dream about similar trips in the Himalayas or for that sake any other mountain range.

A chaotic beginning

A new mail arrives in my mailbox from Lars Gundersen, owner of Kipling Travel. It worries me and I have to call him. He sounds very stressed and says shortly, "Tibet has been completely closed at least in May and possibly also in June. We will have to activate plan E. But at the moment I have more than a hundred individual tours to change."

Our most recent plan was to travel to Nepal in 3 days on May 14th to start our trip by acclimatising to the altitude on some almost 6000 metres high peaks in the Langtang Himal just north of Kathmandu. Then, when we were acclimatised, we would continue to Tibet to climb the more than 8000 metres high Shisha Pangma. That was plan D as previous plans had been changed several times due to the developments in the occupied Tibet and the coming olympic games. And the problems of my expedition are actually small compared to the troubles Lars is having rearranging travels for all his costumers going to Tibet.

One year before this incident I agreed to become expedition leader on the Kipling expedition going to Cho Oyu, with its 8201 metres the worlds sixth highest mountain. We were supposed to take the technically easy route from north in Tibet. That was plan A. I was looking much forward to climb an 8000 metres peak once again. Last time I climbed to that altitude was on Everest in 2000. It had been far to long. But as the expedition was closing up the troubles in Tibet escalated. The upcoming Olympic Games meant prestige for the chinese and they did not appreciate the demonstrations for a free Tibet at all. That would ruin the marketing value of the Olympic Games.

The Chinese authorities had the bright idea to bring the olympic flame to the summit of Everet. They expected a lot of unrest as the flame would travel through Tibet to get to the summit. To avoid bad publicity and make it more possible to control the news until 10th of May, where the flame was expected to reach the summit, the area around Everest was closed. Cho Oyu lies very close by and the entrance is by the same valleys. Unfortunately for us, that meant that we were not allowed into the area before 10th of May. That meant acclimatising in Nepal on smaller mountains. And that was our plan B.

But the demonstrations gathered in strength and a complete closure of the Everest region followed. We decided to move the expedition to another 8000 metres peak, Shisha Pangma, not so far away. But shortly after we decided to do the acclimatisation in Nepal as it seemed there would be problems entering Tibet early in the season. That were respectively our plan C and D.

Every time we made a new plan we also made an new emergency plan. That was also the case when we activated plan D. And on the friday before travel-monday, Tibet was completely closed for the month of May. That is the complete spring season for climbing in that part of the Himalayas. This forced us to give up Tibet completely and concentrate on the next plan, an expedition entirely in Nepal.

The activated plan E contained:

- A long trek from the little air strip Lukla in the Khumbu region taking us first south, then east and finally north across several passes on the way.
- Acclimatise by climbing the summit of Mera Peak, 6476 metres
- Trek to Baruntse, 7129 metres, which now was the main goal
- Trek out across the Amphu Laptsa pas, 5850 metres, to the Khumbu area
- Trek back through Khumbu to Lukla

Thus, plan E did not contain any 8-thousand metres peak. We assessed that the 8-thousanders of Nepal were too difficult technically for our group and too dangerous for a commercial expedition ekspedition.

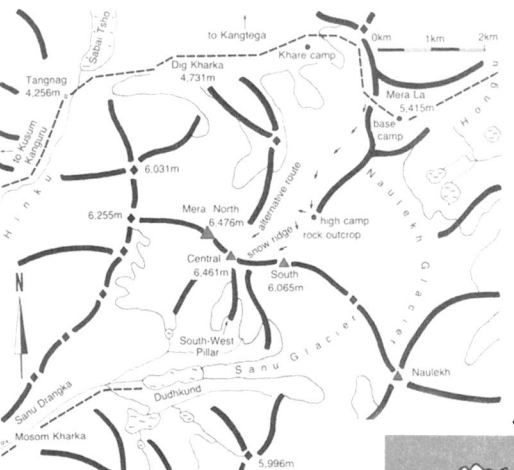

Figure 1: Overview of Mera Peak

Figure 2: Overview of Nepal with the expediton area marked

The travel program shorthly
Copenhagen - Kathmandu
Kathmandu - Lukla
Trek across Pangkonga, Nashing Dingma, Chalem Kharka (2 days incl. acclimatisation trip), Chunbu Kharka, Khote, Tangnag (2 days incl. an acclimatisation trip to Lungsamba Ridge), Khare (Mera basecamp).
Ascent of Mera Central and Mera North during 3 days
Trek via Pokhari to Baruntse basecamp
Climb of Baruntse during 16 days
Trek across Amphu Laptsa basecamp, the pass Amphu Laptsa, Chhukung, Tengpoche, Namche Bazar eventually returning to Lukla.
Lukla - Kathmandu
Kathmandu - Copenhagen

Acclimatisation

The trek to Mera is a fantastic trip in itself. In the course of 5 days we walk through Pangkongma and Nashing Dingma. A very foggy day we traverse a col at 4350 metres before going up through the Hinku valley. Apparently closing and dominating this valley is the steep mountain Tangtse that seemingly overhangs the small village of Tangnag. From there it is only a short day's march to Khare, which is regarded as Mera Basecamp, though it looks like no other basecamp I have visited.

At this time we have only been away for 6 days and have passed a single high col. There we took an extra acclimatisation day to become better accustomed to the low oxygen level at altitude but we are still far from fully acclimatised.

Figure 3: The view up through the Khumbu valley from near to Pangkomgma

Therefore, we spend an extra acclimatisation day around Tangnag walking through dense fog up a ridge against the mountain of Kusum Kanguru. We reach an altitude of around 5000 metres, which will help us when we climb towards Mera in 3 days.

The day after we arrive to Khare where we find a handful of lodges and shops offering the most necessary for climbing Mera. That is if you arrive here without plans to climb Mera Peak and suddenly realise you would like to do just that. However

Figure 4: Camp in Pangkongma

that is not legal as it requires a climbing permit to climb the mountain legally. The permit is inexpensive but it can't be obtained her in Khare. There are probably lots of people who climb Mera Peak without this extended trekking permit.

On our way to Mera Peak the group of six people and our 3 sherpas discus the diffe-

Figur 6: Lejr i Nashing Dingma

rent summits of Mera. Most people climb only Mera Central which is 15 metres lower thant Mera North. But Mera North is said to be much more difficult. Thus most climbers say they climbed Mera without actually being on the highest peak. Our plan is to climb Mera North and it spurs us even more that one of the sherpas starts postu-

Facts about the participants:

From the beginning there were 6 participants in Kipling Travels Baruntse exp. 2008:

- Steen Ulriksen, who unfortunately had to turn around on Mera Peak and travel back to Denmark due to problem with an old very severe leg injury.
- Jesper Johannesen, who reached the summit of both Mera peaks in spite of severe stomach problems. But before attempting Baruntse he had to travel home as his stomach continued to give him problems and he became weaker and weaker.
- Anny Kvithyll, who reached the summit of Mera North.
- Jens Trolle Nielsen, who reached all attempted summits (Mera Central, Mera North, Baruntse II and Baruntse).
- Martin Cederkrantz, who reached all attempted summits.
- Expedition leader, Bo Belvedere Christensen, who reached all summits.

Figure 7: Jesper on one of our acclimatisation climbs

Figure 8: Head shaped rock pillar near Chalem Kharka

Figure 9: The beautiful and difficult mountain TangTse

lating that it will take several days longer to climb that peak. We can't accept that and our sirdar, the leader of the sherpas, cuts the discussion and says, "of course we can climb it and it wont take any longer, but we might find it a bit difficult."

The day after staying in Khare - Mera Basecamp - we climb onto the Mera glacier and crosses it flatly against Mera La (Mera Col), where our next camp is situated at 5400 metres. The camp is situated just below the col on the East side as the col itself is icy and very windy.

Likewise is also Mera High Camp hidden away. Situated at approximately 5800 metres behind a small rocky ridge that shields against the wind and provides rock shelves for the tents, it is a place that provides for the necessary rest before the summit attempt. But both Mera La and Mera High Camp are dirty places with human debris left lying in piles all around.

The claim that we should spend another week to gain the summit of Mera North is completely ridiculed the next day. Jens, Martin, Jesper and I climb on the summit day the 700 metres from Mera High Camp to Mera Central and afterwards to the North Summit without major difficulty. Lhakpa, our sirdar, is the only to rush it a little too much. He ends up with one leg into a deep hole while testing a snow bridge across a small crevasse.

The route up to Mera Central is actually rather spectacular as we cross a small crevasse at the edge of the glacier. Through the crevasse we have a view to the whole valley, we walked in a few days ago.

Figure 11: Hanging glacier on TangTse

It is no technical challenge and provides us with a nice view. The last 15 metres is a steeper snow and ice wall. With a fixed rope it doesn't offer any big challenge either. After a short while we leave the central summit and less than an hour after we stood on the first summit,

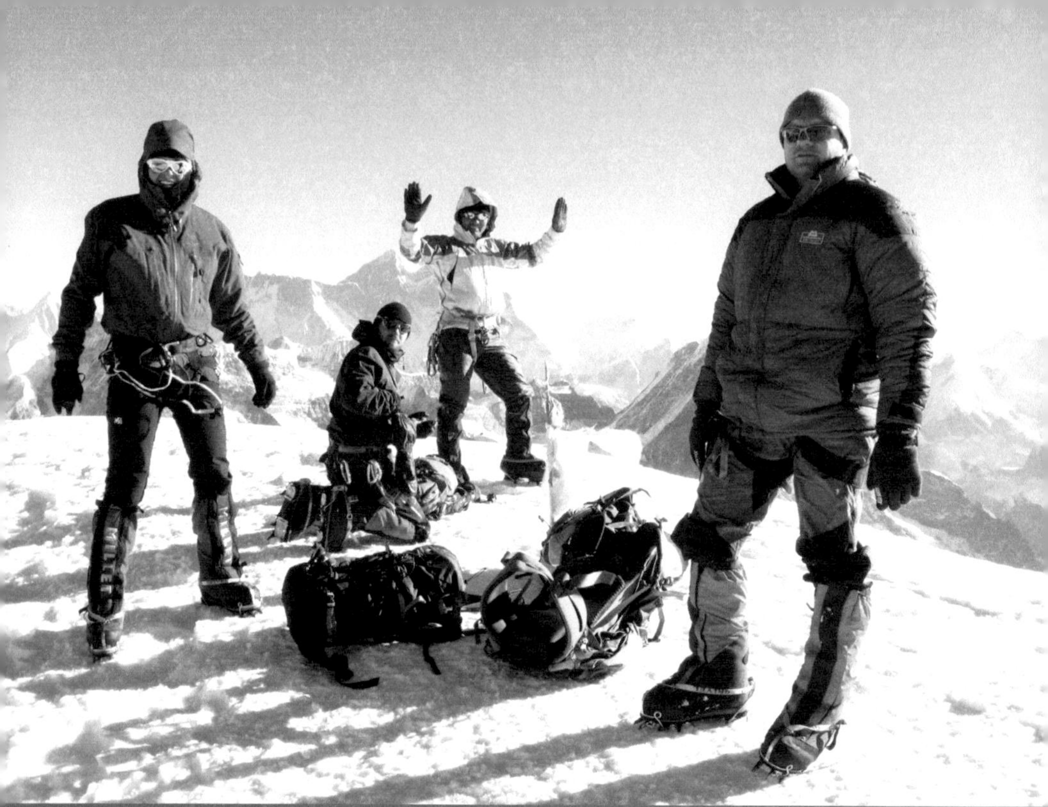
MILLET
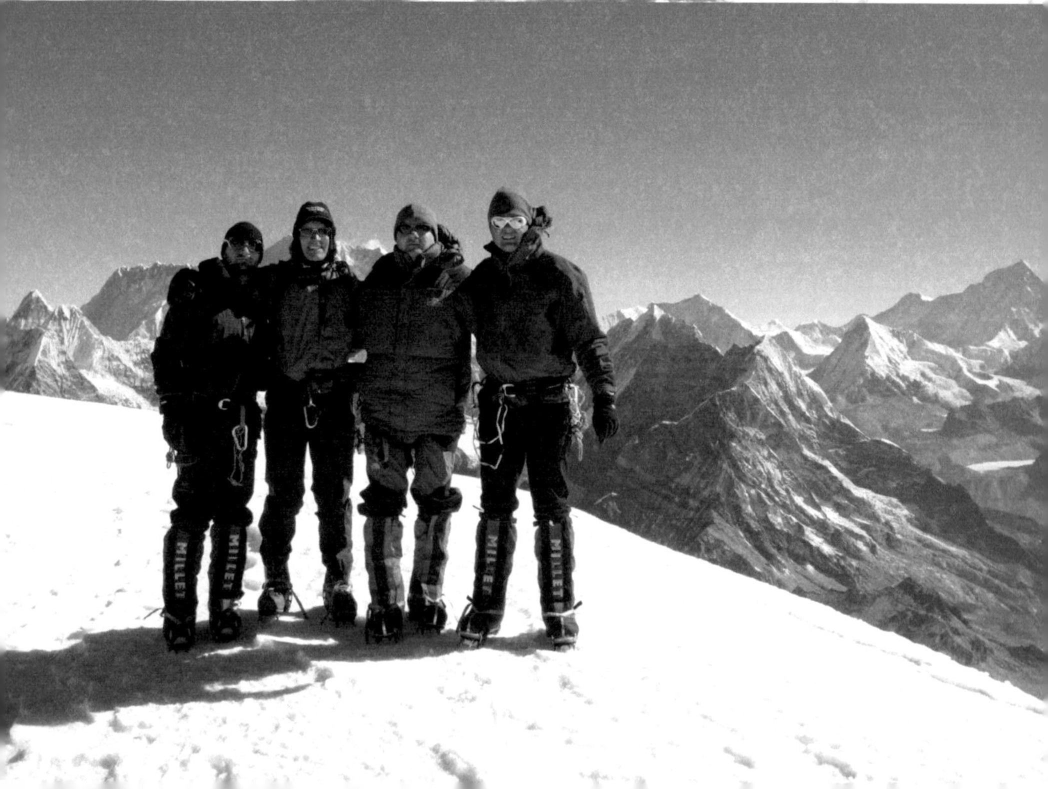
MILLET
MILLET
MILLET

Figure 12 side 15 : The two highest Mera summits, the central summit in the middle, North to the right
Figure 13 side 15: On route up the last part of the Mera glacier
Figure 14 side 16: Many glacier have a steep edge. The Mera glacier is no exception
Figure 15 side 16: A few hours after the start from Mera High Camp
Figure 16 side 17: Martin, Jens, and Jesper on Mera with Everest behind and Baruntse to the right
Figure 17 side 17: Jesper at the crevasse below the summit wall on Mera Central
Figure 18 side 18: Lhakpa dancing for victory on Mera Central
Figure 19 side 18: Martin, Bo, Jesper and Jens on Mera North. Baruntse behind us to the right
Figure 20 side 19: Anny and Dachhamba on the last part against the summit
Figure 21 side 19: Bo and Anny on the summit of Mera North
Figure 22 side 20: Martin and Jens on the way to West Col during a snow shover
Figure 23 side 20: Martin on the snow covered moraine with Baruntse and Baruntse II in the background

we arrive at the North summit. Now we allow Lhakpa to make the gesture of victory. When he did so on the central summit, we pointed at Mera North and told him, "over there you can claim victory, not here."

Anny and Steen starts out a while after us in the morning. Steen must accept defeat soon after. He has an issue with his leg that has deteriorated since the day we started. When he's going steeply upwards he's in great pain and he has troubles maintaining his balance. He returns to camp. Anny is not so fast but continues steadily against the summit.

Martin, Jens and Jesper leaves the summit while Lhakpa and I wait for Anny. But we don't have to wait for long. Soon she appears below Mera Central along with another sherpa, Dachhamba. They have seen our trail beneath and around the central summit and they head directly for the highest peak. We greet her just below the last steep part and share the road the last bit and arrive once again on the North Summit.

The view from the summit is magnificient with sights of Kangchenjunga, that stands at the extreme Eastern border of Nepal around 200 km away. The Everest group is close by and so is beautiful Ama Dablam, which i climbed in 1988. But most important is the first view of the primary goal of the expedition, the 7129 metres high Baruntse.

Figure 24: Baruntse basecamp. Behind is West Col in the center of the picture and Baruntse poking its head into the clouds to left. The smaller peak also with cloudy summit is Baruntse II.

Baruntse

Two days later we arrive in Baruntse Basecamp, that lies at a cosy spot by a small lake of glacial melt water. According to the map, the glacier from Baruntse and Hiunchuli should reach the edge of the lake, but it seems like it's many years ago since it did. There is half an hour's march up to the closest edge of the glacier. The closest edge is at the same time the route up towards West Col, the way to the upper slopes of Baruntse and the Southeast ridge of the mountain, the route we are to attempt.

Figure 25: West Col, where the route crossed just to the right of the leftmost rocks.

After a rest, the first actual rest day on the expedition, we spend one day climbing to the West Col at 6150 metres. The last part to the col is pretty steep but one of the sherpas has placed a fixed rope in advance. Safe with a jumar on the

Figure 26: The view towards Makalu from camp 1

rope the climb to the col is relatively easy. But as it starts to snow the jumar looses grip. Once I see Jens take a small slip down the rope, but he stops a few metres lower.

This first time we are somewhat short of breath due to the altitude. A little clumsy due to lack of oxygen one of us stumbles over some rocks. They fall and doesn't stop before they reach the glacier. Luckily the rope traverses a little and no one climbs right below us. We stay up in the altitude for a while to accustom the body to the low oxygen levels. We also leave some equipment for camp 1.

Next day we move up to spend the night in camp 1, which is close to West Col on the glacier up there. Despite a heavy backpack with all the equipment for summit attempt I reach the col 50 minutes faster than yesterday. A promising acclimatisation rate.

After the night Martin, Jens and I make the trail to camp 2 plowing through a thick layer of new snow. The route goes through a small icefall area but without any major difficulties we reach a small

Figure 27: Jens and Martin at camp 1 on the West Col

plateau at 6400 metres altitude. After a little digging around we find the remains of a camp. On the way down we meet the sherpas coming up from basecamp with tents and other stuff to establish camp 2. We return to basecamp for a rest before the summit attempt.

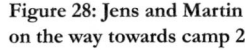

Figure 28: Jens and Martin on the way towards camp 2

The days feels long in basecamp while we wait to be rested enough for the summit push. Actually we feel fresh, but I know from experience that the moment you put on the big backpack and start climbing you feel the fatigue. We need to rest at least two days.

But as we start on May 8th we feel strong and the acclimatisation is very well advanced. The trip to camp 1 goes even faster than last time, and the next day the going up to camp 2 is very relaxed with an increase in altitude of only 250 metres. I have tried to convince

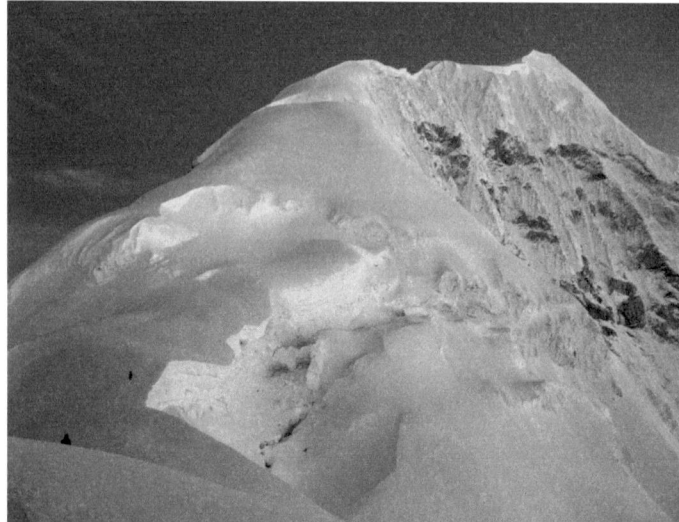

Figure 29: Climbers from our group on their way at dawn

the sherpas that camp 2 should be placed higher. But they haven't been responsive to my arguments. Later we find that I'm actually right about this.

On May 10th we leave camp 2 at 3.30 in the morning bound for the summit. There are a few crevasses to cross just after the camp, but another team has already passed and placed some

Figure 30: The summit attempt takes place in sunny weather with only a few clouds

fixed ropes on the short vertical passage. The rest of the route to the col between Baruntse and the lower Baruntse II (6735 metres) is relatively easy.

From here a huge whaleback of a ridge stretches in a large arc up towards the summit that we believe to see from here. Very often the foreshortened view fools the eye and the climber end up disappointed as the distance to the summit seems to grow. Often the real summit hides behind one or more foresummits. But according to the sherpas it is actually the main summit that we see from the col in 6550 metres altitude.

We continue up the ridge in the first daylight, a fantastic morning, a promising morning. But actually, after climbing only around 400 metres of altitude problems begin to loom over us. The sun is intense and has now been baking the snow for some hours. The snow

24

has become soft and unstable. Climbing up a steep slope we cross a small crevasse, the sides of which crumble under our weight. Fortunately we have placed a fixed rope here and nothing happens. But just above Lhakpa and I try to follow a sharp snowridge that

Figure 31: Starting from the col between Baruntse and Baruntse II

completely disintegrates below us. On both sides we look into deep chasms, especially the East side of the ridge is frightening. Most of the soft ice we try to negociate is stacked on top of nothing as the ridge is actually overhang on that side. With the lack of anything trusthworthy

Figure 32: Jens on fixed ropes at around 6600 metres. Baruntse II just behind him to the left

to fix a belay and runners to it looks very dangerous. We decide that today is not the day and turn around in 6940 metres altitude.

Weak, dehydrated and disillusioned we reach back to camp 2. Martin, Jens and I decide to stay and attempt to ascend Baruntse II tomorrow. We drink huge amounts of liquid and eat as much as possible. But during the day, rest is not easy inside the tent as the temperature reaches 50 degrees celcius. It is a paradox as outside there is a little wind, chill enough to make it difficult to stay warm.

Next morning, not very early, we climb up to the col between Baruntse and Baruntse II once again. From there we follow a ridge, sometimes rather steeply, past some rocky outcrops. We stay a little below the ridge as a view looking back reveals it to be overhanging 5 to 6 metres. Before we arrived to climb I read about the first ascent of Baruntse in 1954. During that a section of 60 metres broke of the snowy ridge when they touched the beginning of it. By sheer luck nobody was hurt, but the ridge here looks very much

Figure 33: Anny and Dachhamba on fixed ropes

like the one on "big" Baruntse. I simply don't trust this ice cake. Cautiously we move ahead. We pass some rocky steps where the ridge steepens but nothing that seriously hinders our passage.

A couple of hours after starting the climb the

Figure 34: The scary soft ridge where we turned around in 6900 metres

ridge begins to level out, we increase the speed and soon after we take the last steps onto the summit of Baruntse II, our consolation prize. At the moment we feel happy, but it not what we came for.

Later that day we descend all the way to basecamp. Here they have kept an eye on us and they know we have been on the summit of the smaller Baruntse. We are offered nice food and a lot to drink and recounts the story of the ascent to Anny. She felt to weak yesterday to accompany us in the ascent to day and I feel sorry for her. Imagine this might be it, we might not get another chance.

Figure 35 page 27: The group in Baruntse Basecamp before the summit attempt

Figure 36 page 27: Baruntse II as seen through telephoto lens from Basecamp

Figure 37 page 28: Jens and Martin in the small icefall between camp 1 and 2

Figure 38 page 28: On the way up the Southeast ridge of Baruntse on beautiful morning

Figure 39 page 29: Jens on the way to Baruntse

Figure 40 page 29: Martin takes a deserved brake beneath a serac wall on the way to Baruntse

Figure 41 page 30: Anny and Dachhamba on their way with Makalu in the background

Figure 42 page 30: The big drop to the valley where Basecamp is located

Figure 43 page 31: Going up the thin edge of the ridge on Baruntse at 6800 metres

Figure 44 page 31: Martin on his way up the ridge of Baruntse II. The trail leads back to the col between Baruntse II and Baruntse. The beautiful summit of Ama Dablam looms in the background

Figure 45 page 32: Martin and Jens near the summit of Baruntse II. "Big" Baruntse behind

Figure 46 page 32: The author, Bo Belvedere Christensen, on the summit of Baruntse II. Both Makalu and Makalu II is seen in the background

Figure 47 page 33: The big unstable ice cake that made us abandon the summit on Baruntse

Figure 48 page 33: Afternoon clouds are covering the valley but not the lakes to the left of which Basecamp is located

G oing home or?

After the summit attempts Jens and I climb a small peak of 5900 metres just above basecamp. It is a climb that indicates to us that we are tired after the long expedition. When we fail to maintain our foothold in the loose rocks in the moraine, we completely run out of breath. But after a couple of hours of exhausting climbing we reach the summit and hopefully the nice view to Baruntse. The weather is acting up; clouds have come up and

Figure 49: Climbers as small dots on their way up the summit ridge of Baruntse

I don't get the photo of Baruntse that i hoped.

Actually, the return journey has been advanced, so we don't have to wait another week in Basecamp. But suddenly, two nights after our return from Baruntse II, Lhakpa enters the dining

Figure 50: A beautiful evening in Basecamp and a new chance to get to the summit

tent and says: "I need your decision on a serious matter." Damn it, I think, what is wrong? But, nothing is wrong; Some of the sherpas from an english expedition have seemingly had colder conditions and have succeded placing a fixed rope beyond the dangerous spot, where we stopped. Lhakpas question is whether we feel strong enough to climb directly from Basecamp to camp 2 in one day - or rather the English camp 2, which is exactly where I wanted camp 2 to be; in the col between Baruntse and Baruntse II. But we will have to attempt the summit early the day after. Need I say that the answer was a loud "YES." There is nothing we would rather do than have another go at the summit. And with the summit camp right where I wanted it, I find the chance of succes growing.

The next day we take the long climb of 1100 metres carrying all the food and gear we need for the 2 days we have left for the attempt. I've had stomach aches for a couple of

Figure 51: Lhakpa carrying his backpack with straps and band across his forehead

days and suffers from stomach cramps. I don't feel fresh at all, but I gather the strength and convince myself that I will be fine tomorrow. Usually I have a very strong stomach and need not worry, but later I find that I had an infection of amoeba and that it required heavy 10 day cure of ciproflaxin to stop it.

Figure 52: A lightly clouded morning we start our second summit attempt on Baruntse

The weather is not very good either, the last hours against the camp we climb in drifting snow and in the col there is an icy wind. Maybe it feels worse due to our tired condition after the long climb up here and the due to the long and exhausting expedition with many summit attempts. But as we get inside the tents we stop caring about all that. We melt the snow we need for water and eat a lot.

Unfortunately, Anny doesn't make it all the way up here. Such a compressed program doesn't fit her very well. Given a little more time Anny can cope with the challenge but when shes forced to keep going and doesn't have time for a lot of breaks, she wont make it. This is our last chance and the time frame is very short, but I will miss her up there.

What actually happens next morning, I don't know. But the sherpas forget to wake us up like they usually do. That makes for a late start at around 5 o'clock without anything to eat and just a little sip of water to drink.

Figure 53: Lhakpa and Pemba, two faithful helpers

I start last from the camp plagued by nausea and with aching stomach. Nevertheless, I catch up with the others after a short while. We pass all the sections, the gently sloping starting wall, the large serac wall, the first sharp ridge with the traversing crevasse. De-

Figure 54: The ridge shortly before our previous high point

spite our late start we still reach our previous high point early. And exactly as we are told there is a fixed rope on the dangerous section and seemingly it continues further on.

Well beyond the first steep passage we can see that Lhakpa is struggling. Normally I would be up there to help him but I'm obviously weakened today. I think about how, on the 8 thousand metres peaks, I have been out in front to break the trail. Today I'm just a tired climber in pain, hoping to be strong enough to summit.

The sherpas from the English team hadn't gone this far, there is no fixed ropes here. They managed the delicate passage further down, but up here they stopped for some reason. And there are more sections that require a fixed rope if we are to climb this with a decent safety margin. Luckily the cloudy weather has continued to today. It is not at all like last time, where the heat melted the snow and made it dangerous. We just hope it doesn't close in completely so we won't see a thing from the summit - if we get there.

There are a few section on the snow ridge where we have to stay some way down on the west side. The top of the ridge is clearly not supported by anything and even though the snow is hard today, it could still break away. Lhakpa has placed the rope a couple of metres from the edge, but a littel further on when I turn around and look back, I conclude that even there we were not completely safe. But when I realise this everyone has passed the critical point safely. We just have jo take care on the trip down.

After some hours of hard work we pass a longer steep section and following this is a broad, flat ridge that only has a small steep section in the top. Could that be ... I dare not believe it but it really looks like the summit is right there. No larger obstacles between us and it. We only have to ascend around 50 metres further then we will be there.

I forget everything about my aching stomach, accelerate past the others to reach Lhakpa just before he disappears from sight beyond the edge. I can't wait any longer, I must know if this is really the summit. When I get to the edge I can see I'm almost there. There is around 50 metres more, not up but along an easy slope. I wait for the others while Lhakpa and another of our sherpas continue to the real summit.

The last steep slope that I have just climbed takes a while for Jens and Martin. It is obvious that they are having a hard time now. They have to take a lot of short rests to make it up this last physically hard section. Jens arrive at the edge and I take some movie shots of him while he climbs over the edge. But he's to short of breath to answer my questions, he only answers in monosyllables.

A short while later Martin arrives as well and we can share the road the last few metres to the highest point. Though we are tired our spirits are high and we shout "Yes, we did it anyway." In spite of all the challenges and the time that is running out, we are successful. Lhakpa ascertains that we don't get to close to the edge. A moment ago he lost both his ice axes. He stuck them in the snow when he arrived and a moment later the ridge broke of right in front of him where he put his ice axes. Scary climbing right to the summit.

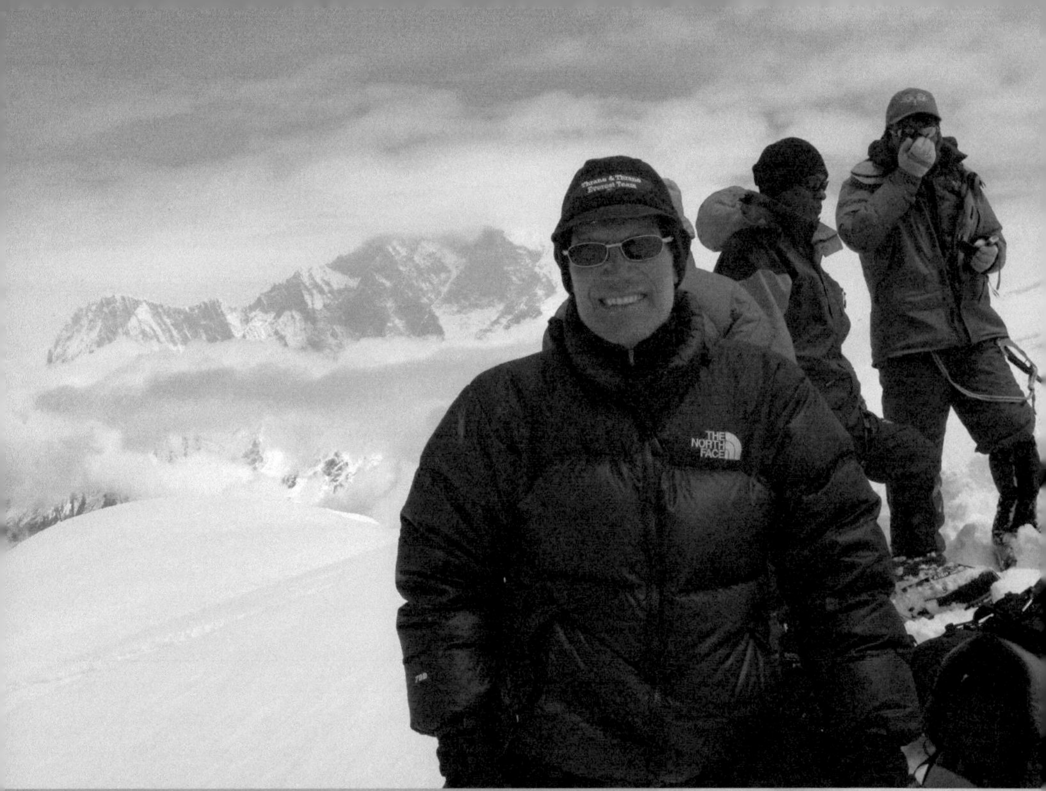
Thrane & Thrane
Everest Team
THE NORTH FACE

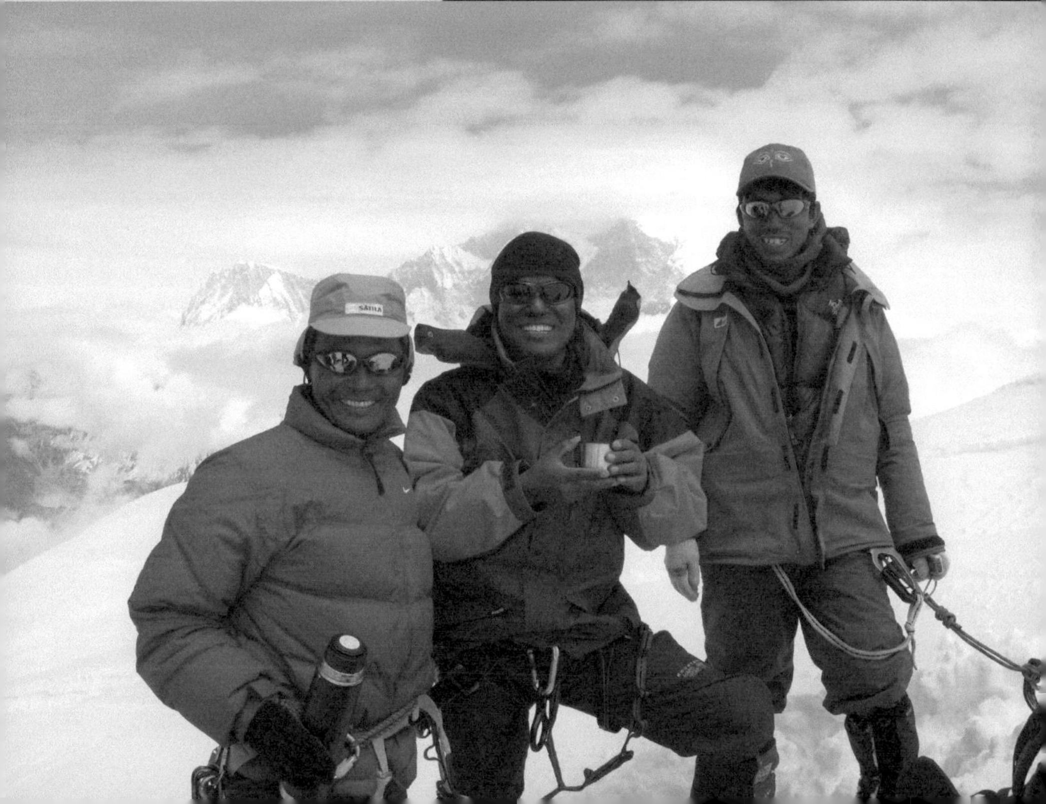

Closing the ring

The trip to basecamp is eventless. It's just a long hard trip - especially as we decide to make it all the way from summit to basecamp that same day. The summit camp invites to a break for a lot to drink and a little to eat. After that we continue to camp 1 in the West Col. Here we are met by the English team who congratulates us with the successful ascent. Clearly, everyone knows that we have been up there, we know that they have been following us through binoculars from basecamp - actually the sharpest eyes could spot us with the naked eye.

The English team is on their summit push and will continue to the summit camp tomorrow. Two japanese who have been on individual expeditions have joined forces and are here as well with the same intention. In the light of our succes they are all optimistic. In two days we will all know for certain whether they are up to the challenge.

Two days later after resting a day in basecamp we are taking down our camp. At the same time we are watching the English and Japanese teams attempt. To begin with they are far ahead of the timeschedule from our successful attempt, but as they are getting closer to the summit the speed decreases markedly. Around eleven o'clock we have to leave camp in order to reach our evening goal, a camp below the Amphu Laptsa pass that we must cross tomorrow. Thus, we get no certainty of the other teams' success, but it looks promising with several small dots making their way up the last steep passage just around an hour from the summit.

The trip across the 5845 metres high Amphu Laptsa is a very special experience. We walk steeply up to a glacier on the south side of the pass. The glacier is divided into several terrasses separated by an 8 to 10 metres vertical wall. We climb onto the lowermost of these

Figure 55 page 39: Just passed the gap in the snowridge marked by a traversion crevasse

Figure 56 page 39: Martin on the short vertical section of the ridge

Figure 57 page 40: We believe to be looking at the summit at the right, but nothing is certain

Figure 58 page 40: Martin on the last part of the snow ridge

Figure 59 page 41: The broad final ridge, now we know we will make it

Figure 60 page 41: Bo, Martin and Jens on the summit of Baruntse

Figure 61 page 42: Jens on the summit of Baruntse

Figure 62 page 42: Martin on the summit of Baruntse

Figure 63 page 43: Bo on the summit of Baruntse, in the background the Everest group looms

Figure 64 page 43: Three happy sherpas on the summit of Baruntse: Lhakpa, Pemba and Balbadur

terasses and establish a fixed rope to help the porters. With their tennisshoes and third grade boots they need help to get up this slippery path. From here we walk up along the edge of the glacier in the wet snow from yesterday. Some of the porters have tied strings around their shoes or boots. This works a little like crampons but they still slide around in the steep wet snow.

It is quite different as soon as we reach the pass. The sun is strong now and has melted the snow. We take a rest sitting on the rocks and enjoying the view towards both the Hinku valley and the Khumbu area. Amphu Laptsa is one of the few places that links the Baruntse/Hinku valley area to the Khumbu area. But no matter which route you choose it will be a challenge for the porters with their lousy footwear and carrying a huge load.

Figure 65: Some of the climbers from the english team on the last steep part of the climb to Baruntse. The summit is the high point in the left of the view

Later that same day we are already deep down in the Khumbu area. We spend the night at 5150 metres in a nice valley behind the moraine from the glacier descending from Lhotse.

Next day takes us out of real high altitudes. This evening we sleep below 5000 metres for the first time since we went up from Mera Peak Basecamp. The night is spent in Dingboche and the following days takes us along broad trails through the Khumbu area and past the beautiful buddhist monastery of Tengboche.

Seven days after reaching the summit of Baruntse the long trek across Amphu Laptsa and through Khumbu ends in Lukla. Thereby we have closed a gigantic ring, a trek around the mountains, through 4 large valleys, climbing 3 major summits on the way. A truly fantastic trip with lots of experiences, challenges and success.

I'm not sorry at all for not getting to one of the 8000 metres peak I was longing for. I have long time since found it strange that I have climbed two 8000 metres peaks and several above 6000 metres, but not one single 7000 metres peak.

With this expedition that hole is closed in the most appropriate way.

Expedition Summary

Total duration from April 14th (travelling from Copenhagen) to June 28th 2008 (arrival back in Denmark), in total 44 days. From Lukla to Lukla: April 17th to May 23rd.

Mountains ascended:

Mera Central, 6461 metres:
- Jens Trolle Nielsen
- Martin Cederkrantz
- Jesper Johannesen
- Bo Belvedere Christensen

Mera North, 6476 metres:
- Jens Trolle Nielsen
- Martin Cederkrantz
- Jesper Johannesen
- Anny Kvithyll
- Bo Belvedere Christensen

Baruntse 2, 6735 metres:
- Jens Trolle Nielsen
- Martin Cederkrantz
- Bo Belvedere Christensen

Baruntse, 7129 metres:
- Jens Trolle Nielsen
- Martin Cederkrantz
- Bo Belvedere Christensen

Mera Peak camps and altitude differences:

Place	Altitude	Alt. difference
Mera Peak Basecamp (Khare)	5000m	
Mera La	5400m	400m
Mera High Camp	5800m	400m
Mera North Summit	6476m	676m

Figure 66: Baruntse BC by night
Figure 67: Dachhamba on his way to Amphu Laptsa with the terraced glacier behind
Figure 68: A view from Amphu Laptsa
Figure 69: The view towards where we are descending from the Amphu Laptsa pass
Figure 70: At Dingboche we are passing below the extremely beautiful mountain Ama Dablam, my first Himalayan summit
Figure 71: Sometimes you get so tired ... Anny at the end of the expedition

Baruntse camps and altitude difference:

Place	Altitude	Alt. difference
Baruntse Basecamp	5400m	
Camp 1	6100m	700m
Camp 2a	6400m	300m
Camp 2b	6500m	100m
Baruntse II	6735m	335m (from C2a)
Baruntse	7129m	629m (from C2b)

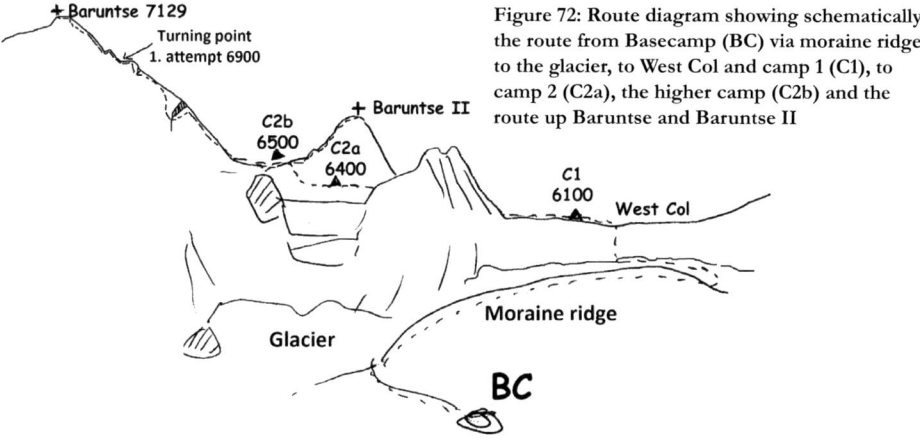

Figure 72: Route diagram showing schematically the route from Basecamp (BC) via moraine ridge to the glacier, to West Col and camp 1 (C1), to camp 2 (C2a), the higher camp (C2b) and the route up Baruntse and Baruntse II

The altitude diagram with its 4 summits above 6000 metres clearly shows:

1. The ascent of Mera Peak.
2. First acclimatisation trip to camp 1 and 2.
3. First summit attempt on Baruntse and the successful ascent of Baruntse II.
4. The ascent of Baruntse, where the curve reaches a little above 7000 metres :-)

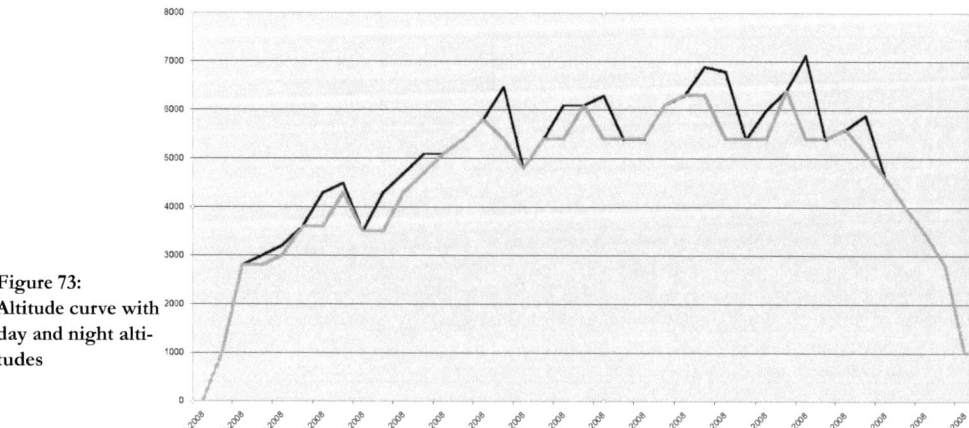

Figure 73: Altitude curve with day and night altitudes

Facts on the Author

Bo Belvedere Christensen works as expedition leader for Kipling Travel building on his 30 years of mountaineering experience and 20 years of Himalayan experience with expeditions among others to Ama Dablam, Dhaulagiri, Broad Peak, Gasherbrum I, Everest, Baruntse.

List of the authors achievements on mountains higher than 5000 – not included is "hills" like Kala Patar in Nepal, even if reaching the altitude.

Mountain	Altitude	Region	Year	Remarks
Elbrus	5641 metres	Caucasus	2006	
Nevado Pisco	5850 metres	Peru	1984	First danish ascent
Kilimanjaro	5895 metres	Tanzania	2007	
Toqllaraju	6032 metres	Peru	1984	First danish ascent
Lobuje Peak	6119 metres	Nepal	1996	
Danga Peak	6450 metres	Nepal	2002	First ascent of the mountain
Mera Peak (North+Central)	6476 metres	Nepal	2008	
Baruntse 2	6735 metres	Nepal	2008	First danish ascent
Huascaran	6768 metres	Peru	1984	
Pandra	6850 metres	Nepal	2002	First ascent of the mountain
Ama Dablam	6856 metres	Nepal	1988	First danish ascent
Aconcagua	6980 metres	Argentina	2007	
Baruntse	7129 metres	Nepal	2008	
Broad Peak	8047 metres	Pakistan	1994	First danish ascent
Gasherbrum I	8068 metres	Pakistan	1998	First danish ascent

Bo had his debut as writer as co-author of "Ama Dablam, an ascent of the most beautiful mountain" (in Danish, Gyldendal 1990), later Bo edited and co-authored "Everest, the dream and the victory" (Jyllandsposten 2000). Bo writes to magazines like "Opdag Verden", "Luxus" and major news papers.

Within the last years Bo has published the following books (so far only in Danish):

- Baruntse – Over 7000 meter i Himalaya, BoD 2008, ISBN 978-87-7691-953-5
- Big E - Fortællingen om Big E Thrane & Thrane Danish Everest Expedition 2000, BoD 2008, ISBN 978-87-7691-354-0
- Ubetrådte tinder - Gennem hvide pletter på landkortet til toppen af jomfruelige toppe i Himalaya, BoD 2008, ISBN 978-87-7691-358-8
- Kilimanjaro - Guide til natur og bestigning, BoD 2009, ISBN 978-87-7691-440-0.
- Vertikalt - Noveller om klatring og bjergbestigning, BoD 2009.
- De Smukke Bjerge - Gasherbrum gruppen i Pakistan, BoD 2010.
- Klatring i Peru - På udfordrende tinder i Andesbjergene, BoD 2011.

Bo gives lectures on mountaineering both as storytelling and in relation to company specific events like customer seminars and sales kick-offs.

Bo writes for and shows his pictures on several websites: Danish Himalayan Society - www.himalaya.dk; the website of his own company K2 adventure - www.k2-adventure.dk; the picture gallery at: gallery.k2-adventure.dk: K2 adventure gives you further information on the lectures and you can download a lecture folder and climbing oriented CV.

Figure 74: Bo Belvedere Christensen in the hot southern France